Progress-Monitoring
Assessments

Grade 1

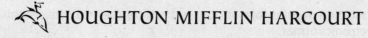

HOUGHTON MIFFLIN HARCOURT

Contents

Progress-Monitoring Assessments

The *Houghton Mifflin Harcourt Journeys* program provides intervention to support children who are having difficulty learning to read. The Progress-Monitoring Assessments provide biweekly checks on children's progress. The fifteen oral tests are administered individually and assess children's mastery of the high-frequency words and skills introduced in the prior two-week period.

Purpose of the Progress-Monitoring Assessments

- To check on a child's growth or problems in learning skills and high-frequency words
- To target learning gaps by using these test results combined with test results from the core instructional program

Skills Tested in the Intervention Program

Tested skills include
- Phonics
- High-Frequency Words
- Fluency and Comprehension

The charts on pages v and vi provide the list of tested skills and high-frequency words. These are the same skills taught in the core instructional program.

Contents of the Progress-Monitoring Assessments

Assessments for	Phonics and Structural Analysis Skills	Phonograms	High-Frequency Words (Words to Know)
Lessons 1–2	Short *a*, short *i* Consonants *n, d, p, f; r, h, /z/s, b, g*	*-it*	and, be, help, play; for, he, look, what
Lessons 3–4	Short *o*, short *e* Consonants *l, x* Inflection *-s* Consonants *y, w, k, v, j*	*-et*	do, funny, no, they; all, does, here, who
Lessons 5–6	Short *u*; review short *a* Consonants *qu, z* Double final consonants and *ck*	*-ack*	friend, good, have, hold; away, come, every, said
Lessons 7–8	Review short *i* and short *o* Blends with *r, l*	*-ip* *-ock*	how, make, of, why; her, now, our, she
Lessons 9–10	Review short *e* and short *u* 2- and 3-letter blends with *s*; final blends	*-ump*	after, read, was, write; eat, give, put, take
Lessons 11–12	Digraphs *th, ch, tch* Base words and *-s, -es, -ed, -ing* Possessives *'s*	*-atch*	far, little, water, where; never, off, out, very
Lessons 13–14	Digraphs *sh, wh, ph* Contractions with *'s, n't* Long *a* (CVC*e*) Soft *c, g, dge*	*-ake* *-ace*	down, fall, open, yellow; over, three, two, watch
Lessons 15–16	Long *i*, long *o*, and long *u* (CVC*e*) Long *o* (CV) Digraphs *kn, wr, gn, mb*	*-ine* *-ite*	eyes, long, or, walk; around, before, light, show

Contents of the Progress-Monitoring Assessments (continued)

Assessments for	Phonics and Structural Analysis Skills	Phonograms	High-Frequency Words (Words to Know)
Lessons 17–18	Long *e* (CV, CVC*e*) Vowel pairs *ee, ea; ai, ay* Final *ng, nk* Contractions *'ll, 'd*	-ean -ink -ay -ain	by, car, don't, sure; sometimes, these, under, your
Lessons 19–20	Vowel pairs *oa, ow* Contractions *'ve, 're* Compound words Short vowel /e /, *ea*	-ow -oat	great, paper, soon, work; more, old, try, want
Lessons 21–22	*r*-Controlled Vowels *ar, or, ore; er, ir, ur*	-ar -ore	few, loudly, night, noise; baby, learning, until, young
Lessons 23–24	Vowel Digraph *oo* (sound in *book*) Syllable Pattern (CVC) Vowel Digraphs/Spelling Patterns for /$\overline{oo}$/: *oo, ou, ew, ue, u, u_e*		again, began, nothing, together; country, earth, soil, warms
Lessons 25–26	Vowel Combinations *ou, ow; oi, oy, au, aw* Base Words/Inflections -*ed, -ing* (CVC*e*, CVC) Long *e* Spelling Patterns *y, ie*		buy, family, myself, please; even, studied, surprised, teacher
Lessons 27–28	Base Words/Inflections -*er, -est*; change *y* to *i* Syllable -*le* Long *i* Spelling Patterns *igh, y, ie* Base Words/Inflections -*ed, -ing, -er, -est, -es*	-ight -y	always, different, happy, stories; cried, heard, large, should
Lessons 29–30	Suffixes -*ful, -ly, -y* Long Vowel Spelling patterns: *a, e, i, o, u* Syllabication (CV) Prefixes *un-, re-*		caught, idea, listen, took; everyone, field, loved, most

Test Organization

- There are fifteen biweekly assessments provided on blackline masters.
- For each assessment there is a teacher page followed by the child's test page with directions for ease of administering and scoring each test.
- Each assessment is divided into sections to test specific skills.
- This booklet also provides directions for administering and scoring each test. Guidelines for interpreting the results of the intervention program and reproducible record-keeping forms are included.

Sections on the Tests

A: Decodable Words This section measures a child's ability to read decodable words independently. The words target phonics and structural elements taught in the last two lessons. Words in each row target skills from a single week's lesson.

Directions: Read each of these words aloud.

sing	think	bank	keep	bean
day	stay	rain	main	he'd

B: High-Frequency Words Items in this section evaluate a child's ability to recognize high-frequency words (Words to Know) taught in a two-week period. Each row assesses knowledge of words taught in a single week's lesson.

Directions: Read each of these words aloud.

by	car	don't	sure
these	sometimes	under	your

Lessons 1–20, C: Reading Sentences measures a child's ability to read sentences accurately. The sentences are a combination of decodable and familiar high-frequency words and become more complex as the year progresses.

Directions: Read each of these sentences aloud.

1. Jen and Ken hop.

2. They hop and play.

3. They get all wet.

Lessons 21–30, C: Oral Reading of paragraphs measures a child's reading fluency, which is a combination of accuracy and rate. A comprehension question is included to evaluate the child's understanding of what is read. Fluency goals are based on below grade-level norms in order to measure progress with intervention instruction. Use grade-level fluency norms, along with observation and program assessment, to determine whether or not a child can transition out of intervention.

Administering the Assessments

Administer each assessment orally to individuals approximately every two weeks. The test should take three to five minutes.

Prepare one test form for children and a teacher's test form for each child being tested. Use it to record the child's responses and scores.

Materials Needed

- Child's test form
- Teacher's test form (one per child being tested)
- Stopwatch or watch or clock with a second hand (Oral Reading only)
- Clipboard (optional)

Keep in Mind

- Find a quiet place to give the test.

- Seat the child on the opposite side of a desk or table so that you can record responses inconspicuously.

- Tell the child that you want to learn how well he or she understands new sounds and words that the group has been learning. Explain that you will write down the child's responses to help you remember them.

- Give directions for each section, modifying them so that the child knows what to do.

- Give the child a reasonable time to respond.

- Stop testing if the child becomes frustrated or is unable to respond.

- Wait until the child has left to score or analyze responses.

To administer Decodable Words, High-Frequency Words (Sections A and B)**, and Reading Sentences** (Section C, Lessons 1–20)**:**

- Ask the child to read each word or sentence aloud.

- Treat each word as a separate item.

- If a word is misread, write what the child said above the word.

- Draw a line through any words that are skipped, and insert words that the child adds. Mark self-corrections with an SC above the word.

To administer Oral Reading (Section C, Lessons 21–30)**:**

- Have a clock or watch with a second hand or a stopwatch available to time the child's reading.

- Explain that the test has two parts. First, you'll listen as the child reads the passage aloud. Then you'll ask a question about it. If the child does not know a word, remind him or her to use the letter-sounds.

- Time the child's reading for 30 seconds.

- If the child reads fewer than two of the first ten words, ask the child to stop. Write *discontinue* on the test form and a zero as the score.

- Draw a line through any mispronounced or omitted words. Write in words that the child inserts. Mark self-corrections with an SC above the word. (Self-corrections and repetitions will *not* be counted as errors.)

- Mark an X on the last word the child reads at the 30-second point.

- Allow the child to read to the end of the passage.

- Ask the comprehension question.

Scoring the Assessments

1. Obtain a child's raw score for each section by determining the number of words read correctly; record the score on the teacher's test form.

   To determine accuracy scores:

   - Treat each word as a separate item.

   - Count mispronunciations, additions, and omissions as errors.

   - Do not count repetitions or self-corrections as errors.

   - Record the number of words read correctly.

   To score fluency for oral reading passages:

   - Determine errors made in reading for 30 seconds, using the guidelines for accuracy above.

   - Determine words read correctly in 30 seconds by subtracting errors from the total words read.

   - Multiply the words read correctly by 2 to determine the number of words read correctly per minute.

   To score the comprehension question:

   - Evaluate the completeness of the child's answer.

   - Give two points for a thorough answer. Give one point for an answer that was not detailed enough or that required prompting. Give no points if the child cannot or did not respond.

2. Use the child's scores to determine if the child is meeting the goals that are given for each section.

3. Use the test data and your observations to decide whether the child should move ahead or needs reteaching.

4. Record each child's scores across assessment periods on the Progress-Monitoring Chart. See the blackline masters on pages xiv–xv.

Interpreting Test Results

Use progress-monitoring test results plus core instruction assessments to make decisions about future intervention instruction. They will help you:

- determine if the child needs additional intervention or can be transitioned back to core instruction only

- evaluate the overall effectiveness of intervention by noting sufficient progress and learning

- adjust skill instruction to address specific learning gaps

Consider how a child's scores compare to the section goals. Decide if the child is benefiting from additional intervention.

☐ **Move Ahead** The child met goals for two or more sections.	☐ **Needs Reteaching** The child did not meet goals for two or more sections.

Adjusting Instruction

Analyze a child's errors and self-corrections in each section to identify problem areas and a starting point for reteaching, review, and extra practice.

- For phonics errors, provide additional word blending activities using word lists that feature target phonics skills. The goal here is for the child to be able to read approximately one word per second.

- For errors in recognizing high-frequency words, supply brief cumulative (approximately ten words) lists of high-frequency words to read and reread with increasing speed and accuracy.

- For improving rate, provide texts at a child's independent reading level for repeated or coached readings.

Test Results and Regrouping

Children in Strategic Intervention take part in the core instruction, activities, and assessments from *Houghton Mifflin Harcourt Journeys*. Test results from the Progress-Monitoring Assessments and Quick Check observations from the lessons indicate whether a child is benefiting from Strategic Intervention. Test results from other *Journeys* assessments provide data to help determine how to regroup children periodically.

Using *Houghton Mifflin Harcourt Journeys* Assessments	
Core Instructional Program Weekly and Unit Tests Benchmark and Fluency Tests	• Measure grade-level skill mastery and growth. • Use cut-off scores and professional judgment to regroup children who need intervention support.
Strategic Intervention Biweekly Progress-Monitoring Assessments	• Measures a child's gains as a result of Strategic Intervention instruction. • Use progress monitoring results as well as observations and program assessments to determine if child needs additional Strategic Intervention or should transition out of intervention or to more intensive intervention.

Progress-Monitoring Chart

Name _____

Teacher _____

School year _____

For each column, enter
+ (the child met the goal) or − (the child did not meet goal)

Progress Monitoring	Date Given	Decodable Words	High-Frequency Words	Reading Sentences	Actions		Comments
					Move Ahead	Needs Reteaching	
Lessons 1–2							
Lessons 3–4							
Lessons 5–6							
Lessons 7–8							
Lessons 9–10							
Lessons 11–12							
Lessons 13–14							
Lessons 15–16							
Lessons 17–18							
Lessons 19–20							

Progress-Monitoring Chart

Name _____

Teacher _____

School year _____

For each column, enter
+ (the child met the goal) *or* – (the child did not meet goal)

Progress Monitoring	Date Given	Decodable Words	High-Frequency Words	Oral Reading (Enter WCPM)	Comprehension	Actions		Comments
						Move Ahead	Needs Reteaching	
Lessons 21–22								
Lessons 23–24								
Lessons 25–26								
Lessons 27–28								
Lessons 29–30								

Progress Monitoring
© Houghton Mifflin Harcourt Publishing Company

Grade 1

Name _____ Date _____

Decodable Words
Goal 8/10   Score _____ / 10

A.

fan	bat	Sam	nap	sad
hit	rip	did	bib	pig

High-Frequency Words
Goal 7/8   Score _____ / 8

B.

and	be	help	play
he	for	look	what

Reading Sentences
Goal 11/13   Score _____ / 13

C.

1. Pam and Dan sit.

2. Pam ran and hid.

3. Did Dan look for Pam?

☐ **Move Ahead** The child met goals for two or more sections.

☐ **Needs Reteaching** The child did not meet goals for two or more sections.

A.

fan	bat	Sam	nap	sad
hit	rip	did	bib	pig

B.

and	be	help	play
he	for	look	what

C.

1. Pam and Dan sit.
2. Pam ran and hid.
3. Did Dan look for Pam?

Name _____ Date _____

Decodable Words

Goal 8/10   Score _____ / 10

A.

log	top	ox	fox	lot
hen	pet	Jed	yet	vet

High-Frequency Words

Goal 7/8   Score _____ / 8

B.

funny	no	they	do
all	does	here	who

Reading Sentences

Goal 10/12   Score _____ / 12

C.

1. Jen and Ken hop.

2. They hop and play.

3. They get all wet.

☐ **Move Ahead** The child met goals for two or more sections.	☐ **Needs Reteaching** The child did not meet goals for two or more sections.

A.

| log | top | ox | fox | lot |
| hen | pet | Jed | yet | vet |

B.

| funny | no | they | do |
| all | does | here | who |

C.

1. Jen and Ken hop.

2. They hop and play.

3. They get all wet.

4

Name _____ Date _____

A. Decodable Words

Goal 8/10   Score _____ / 10

hut	duck	rug	sun	bud
egg	jazz	Zack	bell	quack

B. High-Frequency Words

Goal 7/8   Score _____ / 8

friend	good	have	hold
away	come	every	said

C. Reading Sentences

Goal 10/13   Score _____ / 13

1. Let us run and play.

2. Jack had no luck.

3. He fell in mud!

☐ **Move Ahead** The child met goals for two or more sections.

☐ **Needs Reteaching** The child did not meet goals for two or more sections.

A.

hut	duck	rug	sun	bud
egg	jazz	Zack	bell	quack

B.

friend	good	have	hold
away	come	every	said

C.

1. Let us run and play.
2. Jack had no luck.
3. He fell in mud!

Decodable Words

Goal 8/10   Score _____ / 10

A.

crib	Brad	rip	drip	flip
clock	lot	frog	log	block

High-Frequency Words

Goal 7/8   Score _____ / 8

B.

how	make	of	why
her	now	our	she

Reading Sentences

Goal 20/23   Score _____ / 23

C.

1. Come away on a trip!

2. Pack a bag for a friend.

3. What can a bag hold?

4. Fran will lock it and zip it.

☐ **Move Ahead** The child met goals for two or more sections.

☐ **Needs Reteaching** The child did not meet goals for two or more sections.

A.

crib	Brad	rip	drip	flip
clock	lot	frog	log	block

B.

how	make	of	why
her	now	our	she

C.

1. Come away on a trip!
2. Pack a bag for a friend.
3. What can a bag hold?
4. Fran will lock it and zip it.

Name _____   Date _____

A. Decodable Words

Goal 8/10   Score _____ / 10

skin	stop	went	scat	send
dump	hum	snug	duck	bump

B. High-Frequency Words

Goal 7/8   Score _____ / 8

after	read	was	write
eat	give	put	take

C. Reading Sentences

Goal 18/21   Score _____ / 21

1. Skip can jump and beg.

2. He can stand on his back legs.

3. He can eat a snack.

4. What a funny pup!

☐ **Move Ahead** The child met goals for two or more sections.

☐ **Needs Reteaching** The child did not meet goals for two or more sections.

A.

skin	stop	went	scat	send
dump	hum	snug	duck	bump

B.

after	read	was	write
eat	give	put	take

C.

1. Skip can jump and beg.
2. He can stand on his back legs.
3. He can eat a snack.
4. What a funny pup!

Name _____ Date _____

Decodable Words

Goal 8/10   Score _____ / 10

A.

things	hatched	itching	bath	cloth
patches	match	much	Beth's	chop

High-Frequency Words

Goal 7/8   Score _____ / 8

B.

water	little	where	far
never	off	out	very

Reading Sentences

Goal 21/25   Score _____ / 25

C.

1. Chip is off to catch a moth.

2. He is on a little path.

3. The moth is never far away.

4. Here it comes.

5. Chip catches it!

☐ **Move Ahead** The child met goals for two or more sections.   ☐ **Needs Reteaching** The child did not meet goals for two or more sections.

A.

things	hatched	itching	bath	cloth
patches	match	much	Beth's	chop

B.

water	little	where	far
never	off	out	very

C.

1. Chip is off to catch a moth.

2. He is on a little path.

3. The moth is never far away.

4. Here it comes.

5. Chip catches it!

A. Decodable Words

Goal 8/10   Score _____ / 10

wash	shave	won't	when	Phil
tape	lace	edge	make	cane

B. High-Frequency Words

Goal 7/8   Score _____ / 8

down	fall	open	yellow
watch	over	three	two

C. Reading Sentences

Goal 29/34   Score _____ / 34

1. Shane will bake a yellow cake.

2. She shakes the mix with an egg.

3. Then she puts it in two pans.

4. She sits down to watch it bake.

5. She places the cake down.

6. Let's eat!

☐ **Move Ahead** The child met goals for two or more sections.   ☐ **Needs Reteaching** The child did not meet goals for two or more sections.

A.

wash	shave	won't	when	Phil
tape	lace	edge	make	cane

B.

down	fall	open	yellow
watch	over	three	two

C.

1. Shane will bake a yellow cake.
2. She shakes the mix with an egg.
3. Then she puts it in two pans.
4. She sits down to watch it bake.
5. She places the cake down.
6. Let's eat!

A. Decodable Words

Goal 8/10   Score _____ / 10

fine	knit	wrap	sign	comb
chose	cute	mule	robe	vote

B. High-Frequency Words

Goal 7/8   Score _____ / 8

walk	or	eyes	long
around	before	light	show

C. Reading Sentences

Goal 33/38   Score _____ / 38

1. Do you know how to plant roses?

2. Roses come in red, white, and yellow.

3. Do roses like to climb up vines?

4. They grow tall if they have a lot of light.

5. Make a note to water the roses.

☐ **Move Ahead** The child met goals for two or more sections.

☐ **Needs Reteaching** The child did not meet goals for two or more sections.

A.

fine	knit	wrap	sign	comb
chose	cute	mule	robe	vote

B.

walk	or	eyes	long
around	before	light	show

C.

1. Do you know how to plant roses?

2. Roses come in red, white, and yellow.

3. Do roses like to climb up vines?

4. They grow tall if they have a lot of light.

5. Make a note to water the roses.

A. Decodable Words   Goal 8/10   Score _____ / 10

sing	think	bank	keep	bean
day	stay	rain	main	he'd

B. High-Frequency Words   Goal 7/8   Score _____ / 8

by	car	don't	sure
these	sometimes	under	your

C. Reading Sentences   Goal 39/44   Score _____ / 44

1. We'll bring your friends to the beach.

2. They will see pink sand and clean water.

3. They can swim and play in the waves.

4. We will walk around on the sand.

5. They can put sand in their pails.

6. The main thing is to stay nearby.

☐ **Move Ahead** The child met goals for two or more sections. | ☐ **Needs Reteaching** The child did not meet goals for two or more sections.

A.

sing	think	bank	keep	bean
day	stay	rain	main	he'd

B.

by	car	don't	sure
these	sometimes	under	your

C.

1. We'll bring your friends to the beach.
2. They will see pink sand and clean water.
3. They can swim and play in the waves.
4. We will walk around on the sand.
5. They can put sand in their pails.
6. The main thing is to stay nearby.

Decodable Words

A.
Goal 8/10   Score _____ / 10

goat	snow	we've	grow	goal
oatmeal	bread	spread	head	rowboat

High-Frequency Words

B.
Goal 7/8   Score _____ / 8

great	soon	paper	work
more	old	try	want

Reading Sentences

C.
Goal 41/46   Score _____ / 46

1. Owen! It is now your bath time!

2. Go get your soap and no tricks.

3. Fill the bathtub with water and get in.

4. I don't want to hear moans and groans.

5. You're going to scrub from head to feet.

6. You know you're to soak until you glow!

☐ **Move Ahead** The child met goals for two or more sections.

☐ **Needs Reteaching** The child did not meet goals for two or more sections.

A.

goat	snow	we've	grow	goal
oatmeal	bread	spread	head	rowboat

B.

great	soon	paper	work
more	old	try	want

C.

1. Owen! It is now your bath time!
2. Go get your soap and no tricks.
3. Fill the bathtub with water and get in.
4. I don't want to hear moans and groans.
5. You're going to scrub from head to feet.
6. You know you're to soak until you glow!

A. Decodable Words

Goal 8/10   Score _____ / 10

bark	corn	cart	yard	wore
herd	burn	dirt	fern	hurt

B. High-Frequency Words

Goal 7/8   Score _____ / 8

few	loudly	night	noise
baby	learning	until	young

Oral Reading Have the child read the title and the entire passage. Start timing when the child begins reading. Make an X in the text at 30 seconds.

C.

The Star Birds	3
I am on a baseball team called the	11
Star Birds. My best friend is on the	19
team, too.	21
The Star Birds play rain or shine.	28
Our games start at four at the park.	36
The coach likes to start on time. Fans	44
come to cheer us on.	49
In our first game, I got a fly ball.	58
It was hit hard and whirled at me. I	67
made the play of the game!	73

Comprehension Question

1. *Who are the Star Birds?* (They are a baseball team.)

Fluency Score	Comprehension Score	How to Score Questions
Total words correctly read in 30 seconds X 2	Score _____ /2	2 = full credit answer 1 = partial credit answer
Goal 13–33 WCPM Score _____	Goal = 1/2	0 = incorrect/unanswered

☐ **Move Ahead** The child met goals for two or more sections.	☐ **Needs Reteaching** The child did not meet goals for two or more sections.

A.

bark	corn	cart	yard	wore
herd	burn	dirt	fern	hurt

B.

few	loudly	night	noise
baby	learning	until	young

C.

The Star Birds

I am on a baseball team called the Star Birds. My best friend is on the team, too.

The Star Birds play rain or shine. Our games start at four at the park. The coach likes to start on time. Fans come to cheer us on.

In our first game, I got a fly ball. It was hit hard and whirled at me. I made the play of the game!

Decodable Words

Goal 8/10   Score _____ / 10

A.

wood	shook	took	hook	hood
blue	boot	chew	Lou	tune

High-Frequency Words

Goal 7/8   Score _____ / 8

B.

again	began	nothing	together
country	earth	soil	warms

Oral Reading Have the child read the title and the entire passage. Start timing when the child begins reading. Make an X in the text at 30 seconds.

C.

Lu-Lu, the Poodle	3
My sister Sue and I thought it was	11
time to get a puppy. We read books	19
about many kinds of dogs.	24
One night we heard something	29
outside. The sound was like a whine	36
coming from the front door. We	42
thought Dad was fooling us.	47
Just then a tan poodle flew into	54
the room! She climbed into our laps,	61
licked our faces, and wagged her tail.	68
We love our new puppy, Lu-Lu!	74

Comprehension Question

1. *What happens to the two sisters in this story?* (They finally get a dog.)

Fluency Score	**Comprehension Score**	**How to Score Questions**
Total words correctly read in 30 seconds ____ X 2	Score ____ /2	2 = full credit answer
Goal 13–33 WCPM Score _____	Goal = 1/2	1 = partial credit answer
		0 = incorrect/unanswered

☐ **Move Ahead** The child met goals for two or more sections.	☐ **Needs Reteaching** The child did not meet goals for two or more sections.

A.

wood	shook	took	hook	hood
blue	boot	chew	Lou	tune

B.

again	began	nothing	together
country	earth	soil	warms

C.

Lu-Lu, the Poodle

My sister Sue and I thought it was time to get a puppy. We read books about many kinds of dogs.

One night we heard something outside. The sound was like a whine coming from the front door. We thought Dad was fooling us.

Just then a tan poodle flew into the room! She climbed into our laps, licked our faces, and wagged her tail. We love our new puppy, Lu-Lu!

A. Decodable Words

Goal 8/10   Score _____ / 10

howl	draw	cloud	boil	cause
many	carried	yawning	happy	chief

B. High-Frequency Words

Goal 7/8   Score _____ / 8

buy	family	myself	please
surprised	studied	even	teacher

Oral Reading Have the child read the title and the entire passage. Start timing when the child begins reading. Make an X in the text at 30 seconds.

C.

Owl's Clean House	3
Owl ran around cleaning her house.	9
Then Owl sat down to rest.	15
Piggy was at the door. Owl shouted,	22
"Don't soil my house with mud."	28
Mouse came by. "Mouse, you have	34
mud on your paws," Owl said out loud.	42
"Don't be such a grouch," said	48
Mouse, waving her paw.	52
All Owl could do was frown. Piggy	59
and Mouse cleaned up the mess.	65
Owl cried with joy. What a relief!	72

Comprehension Question

1. *What does Owl try to do in the story?* (She tries to keep her house clean.)

Fluency Score	Comprehension Score	How to Score Questions
Total words correctly read in 30 seconds _____ X 2	Score _____ /2	2 = full credit answer
		1 = partial credit answer
Goal 13–33 WCPM Score _____	Goal = 1/2	0 = incorrect/unanswered

☐ **Move Ahead** The child met goals for two or more sections.	☐ **Needs Reteaching** The child did not meet goals for two or more sections.

A.

howl	draw	cloud	boil	cause
many	carried	yawning	happy	chief

B.

buy	family	myself	please
surprised	studied	even	teacher

C.

Owl's Clean House

Owl ran around cleaning her house.

Then Owl sat down to rest.

Piggy was at the door. Owl shouted,

"Don't soil my house with mud."

Mouse came by. "Mouse, you have

mud on your paws," Owl said out loud.

"Don't be such a grouch," said

Mouse, waving her paw.

All Owl could do was frown. Piggy

and Mouse cleaned up the mess.

Owl cried with joy. What a relief!

Decodable Words

Goal 8/10   Score _____ / 10

A.

happiest	merrier	taller	largest	able
tie	higher	trying	cry	night

High-Frequency Words

Goal 7/8   Score _____ / 8

B.

always	different	happy	stories
across	large	heard	cried

Oral Reading Have the child read the title and the entire passage. Start timing when the child begins reading. Make an X in the text at 30 seconds.

C.

Be Neat When You Eat	5
Tonight I made a mess at the table.	13
Dad said, "Try to be neat when you	21
eat. You don't want to be so messy."	29
What would it be like to be even	37
messier? I might pile my sloppy food	44
into a high hill. But then it would start	53
to spoil and get smellier and smellier.	60
"I don't think I want to be messier	68
after all," I said.	72
"Let's have some pie," said Dad.	78
I ate the pie very neatly!	84

Comprehension Question

1. *What does the child need to do?* (The child needs to stop being a messy eater.)

Fluency Score	Comprehension Score	How to Score Questions
Total words correctly read in 30 seconds _____ X 2 Goal 13–33 WCPM Score _____	Score ____/2 Goal = 1/2	2 = full credit answer 1 = partial credit answer 0 = incorrect/unanswered
☐ **Move Ahead** The child met goals for two or more sections.	☐ **Needs Reteaching** The child did not meet goals for two or more sections.	

A.

happiest	merrier	taller	largest	able
tie	higher	trying	cry	night

B.

always	different	happy	stories
across	large	heard	cried

C.

Be Neat When You Eat

Tonight I made a mess at the table.

Dad said, "Try to be neat when you eat. You don't want to be so messy."

What would it be like to be even messier? I might pile my sloppy food into a high hill. But then it would start to spoil and get smellier and smellier.

"I don't think I want to be messier after all," I said.

"Let's have some pie," said Dad.

I ate the pie very neatly!

Name _____ Date _____

Progress Monitoring
LESSONS 29–30

Decodable Words
Goal 8/10   Score _____ / 10

A.

careful	lady	mainly	useful	lonely
unfair	undo	remake	untie	repair

High-Frequency Words
Goal 7/8   Score _____ / 8

B.

caught	idea	listen	took
loved	most	field	everyone

Oral Reading Have the child read the title and the entire passage. Start timing when the child begins reading. Make an X in the text at 30 seconds.

C.

Billy's Happy Day!	3
Today was a great day at school. I	11
am so happy! I was hopeful Dad would	19
ask me what's new. And he did!	26
"My story was picked as the best	33
one of the week," I replied. "I read it	42
slowly and clearly to the whole class!"	49
"Wonderful!" Mom said. "Billy, can	54
you please reread it to us?"	60
So I read it to them. Mom and Dad	69
were surprised! They told me it was	76
likely the very best story ever.	82

Comprehension Question
1. Why is this a happy day for Billy? (Billy's story is chosen as the best one of the week.)

Fluency Score	Comprehension Score	How to Score Questions
Total words correctly read in 30 seconds ___ X 2	Score ____ /2	2 = full credit answer
		1 = partial credit answer
Goal 13–33 WCPM Score _____	Goal = 1/2	0 = incorrect/unanswered
☐ **Move Ahead** The child met goals for two or more sections.	☐ **Needs Reteaching** The child did not meet goals for two or more sections.	

Progress Monitoring
© Houghton Mifflin Harcourt Publishing Company

29

Grade 1

A.

careful	lady	mainly	useful	lonely
unfair	undo	remake	untie	repair

B.

caught	idea	listen	took
loved	most	field	everyone

C.

Billy's Happy Day!

Today was a great day at school. I am so happy! I was hopeful Dad would ask me what's new. And he did!

"My story was picked as the best one of the week," I replied. "I read it slowly and clearly to the whole class!"

"Wonderful!" Mom said. "Billy, can you please reread it to us?"

So I read it to them. Mom and Dad were surprised! They told me it was likely the very best story ever.